NBA CHAMPIONSHIPS:

↓

1970, 1973

↓

ALL-TIME LEADING SCORER:

↓

PATRICK EWING (1985–2000):

↓

23,665 POINTS

THE NBA:
A HISTORY
OF HOOPS

NEW YORK
KNICKS

THE NBA: A HISTORY OF HOOPS

NEW YORK KNICKS

BY JIM WHITING

CREATIVE EDUCATION   CREATIVE PAPERBACKS

Published by Creative Education
and Creative Paperbacks

P.O. Box 227, Mankato, Minnesota 56002

Creative Education and Creative Paperbacks
are imprints of The Creative Company

www.thecreativecompany.us

Design and production by Blue Design
Printed in the United States of America

Photographs by Corbis (Bettmann, ADREES
LATIF/Reuters, ERIC MILLER/Reuters, Ray
Stubblebine/Reuters), Getty Images (Al Bello/
Getty Images Sport, Andrew D. Bernstein/
NBAE, Nathaniel S. Butler/NBAE, Jim Cummins/
NBAE, Cameron Davidson, James Drake/Sports
Illustrated, Stephen Dunn, FPG, Glenn James/
NBAE, George Long/Sports Illustrated, George
Long/WireImage, Jim McIsaac/Getty Images
Sport, Fernando Medina/NBAE, NBA Photos/
NBAE, Doug Pensinger, Ken Regan/NBAE, Vaughn
Ridley/Getty Images Sport, Wen Roberts/
NBAE, Carl Skalak/Sports Illustrated, Damian
Strohmeyer/Sports Illustrated, Chris Sweda/
Chicago Tribune/TNS), Newscom (RICH KANE/UPI)

Library of Congress Cataloging-in-Publication Data

Names: Whiting, Jim, 1943- author.

Title: New York Knicks / Jim Whiting.

Series: The NBA: A History of Hoops.

Includes bibliographical references and index.

Summary: This high-interest title summarizes
the history of the New York Knicks professional
basketball team, highlighting memorable events
and noteworthy players such as Willis Reed.

Identifiers: LCCN 2017005591 / ISBN 978-1-
60818-854-3 (hardcover) / ISBN 978-1-62832-
457-0 (pbk) / ISBN 978-1-56660-902-9 (eBook)

Subjects: LCSH: 1. New York Knickerbockers
(Basketball team)—History—Juvenile literature.
2. New York Knickerbockers (Basketball
team)—Biography—Juvenile literature.

Classification: LCC GV885.52.N4 W55 2017
/ DDC 796.323/64097471—dc23

CCSS: RI.4.1, 2, 3, 4; RI.5.1, 2, 4; RI.6.1, 2, 3;
RF.4.3, 4; RF.5.3, 4; RH. 6-8. 4, 5, 7

First Edition HC 9 8 7 6 5 4 3 2 1

First Edition PBK 9 8 7 6 5 4 3 2 1

CONTENTS

LEGENDS OF THE HARDWOOD

More than 2,000 bridges help connect **NEW YORK**

NEW YORK'S DUTCH TREAT

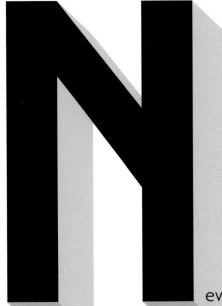

ew York Knicks fans were worried. They were heading into Game 7 of the 1970 National Basketball Association (NBA) Finals. The Knicks were playing the Los Angeles Lakers. Star center

Defensive specialist **WALT FRAZIER** displayed smooth passing and a cool demeanor.

10

Willis Reed had torn a leg muscle in Game 5. He was the league's Most Valuable Player (MVP). The Knicks managed to win that game. But they dropped Game 6. Massive Lakers center Wilt Chamberlain threw down 45 points in a blowout win. Reed's teammates began warming up for Game 7. Reed stayed in the locker room. Doctors gave him shots to numb the pain. "It was a big needle," Reed said. "I saw that needle and I said, 'Holy cow.' And I just held on. I think I suffered more from the needle than the injury."

Reed hobbled onto the court just before the game started. The fans in Madison Square Garden went wild. "The scene is indelibly etched in my mind," said guard Walt Frazier, "because if that did not happen, I know we would not have won the game." Reed scored the first two New York baskets. Those were his only points. Reed's

12

MAKING HISTORY

NAT "SWEETWATER" CLIFTON, FORWARD/CENTER, 6-FOOT-6, 1950-57

Nat Clifton was a high school sensation in Chicago. He served in the army during World War II. After the war, he played for the Harlem Globetrotters. In 1950, he became one of the first African Americans to sign a pro basketball contract. During a game, a rival player yelled a racial slur. Clifton knocked him out. He never had that problem again. "Around Chicago and in the army, I was used to playing with white players, and I could get along," he said. "They [the Knicks] were a great bunch of guys." Clifton averaged 10 points and 8 rebounds a game during his career.

teammates rode the emotional high from his presence. They bolted out to a huge lead. Reed worked on stopping Chamberlain. He scored only four points while Reed was guarding him. The pain finally became too great for Reed to continue. At that point, the Knicks led 61–37. They went on to win 113–99. Frazier finished with 36 points, 19 assists, and 7 rebounds. "Willis provided the inspiration, I provided the devastation," Frazier said. "That was the championship, the one great moment we had all played for," Reed added. It was the Knicks' first NBA title.

T he team dated back to 1946. New York joined the Basketball Association of America (BAA). Naming the team was easy. "We all put a name in a hat, and when we pulled them out, most of them said Knickerbockers," said team official Fred Podesta. The name referred to early Dutch settlers in New York. Their pants were called

The Knicks selected **HARRY GALLATIN** with their first-ever draft pick in 1948.

knickerbockers. They were rolled up to just below the knees. But the name wouldn't fit into newspaper headlines. It was too long. It was quickly shortened to Knicks.

T he Knicks played in the BAA's first game. They defeated the Toronto Huskies, 68–66. The team went 33–27 that season. But it lost in the second round of the playoffs. Then local coach Joe Lapchick took over. The Knicks compiled winning marks the next two seasons. They made early playoff exits both times. The BAA merged with the National Basketball League (NBL) in 1949. The new league became the NBA. Even though no starter was taller than 6-foot-6, the Knicks did well. "Everyone knew his role," said center Harry Gallatin. "We played true team ball." The Knicks advanced to the Eastern Division finals that season. They played in the NBA Finals the next three seasons. Unfortunately, they lost each time.

THE KNICKS' GOLDEN ERA

Lapchick guided the team into the playoffs the next two years as well. But he was under too much stress. He had to retire during the 1955–56 season. Lapchick's exit started a long period of

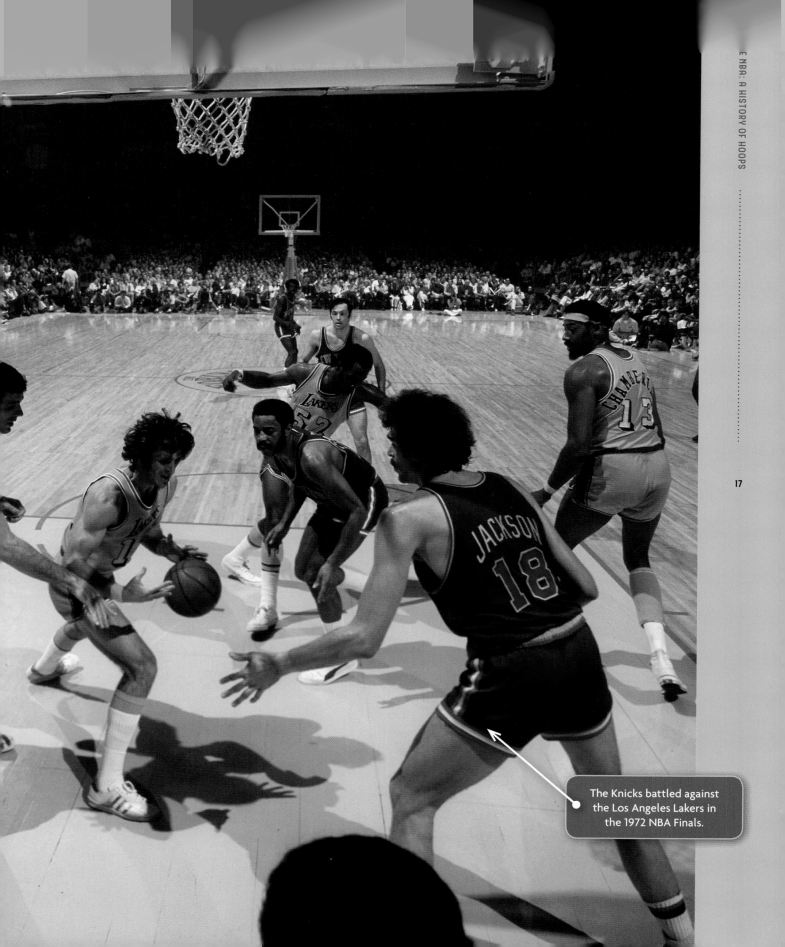

17

The Knicks battled against the Los Angeles Lakers in the 1972 NBA Finals.

decline. In the next 10 years, the Knicks had only one winning record. A highlight came during the 1964–65 season. Reed won the Rookie of the Year award. "The left-handed Reed presented a problem for opposing defenders," notes the *NBA Encyclopedia*. "He had the bulk and the touch to play inside, but he was also deadly with his soft jump shot from up to 15 feet away." Reed couldn't win games by himself, though. The team continued to struggle. Facing yet another losing season midway through 1967–68, the Knicks brought in coach William "Red" Holzman. Holzman had the same team-first belief as Lapchick. The Knicks soon became equally as successful. In Holzman's first full season, New York won a best-ever 54 games. The Knicks lost to the Boston Celtics in the divisional finals, four games to two.

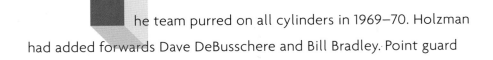

T he team purred on all cylinders in 1969–70. Holzman had added forwards Dave DeBusschere and Bill Bradley. Point guard

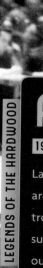

A GOLDEN MOMENT

1970 NBA FINALS, GAME 5, LOS ANGELES LAKERS AT NEW YORK KNICKS, MAY 4, 1970

Late in the first quarter, the Lakers had a 10-point lead. Knicks center Willis Reed tried to drive around Lakers center Wilt Chamberlain. He tripped and tore a leg muscle. His teammates had trouble scoring. At halftime, forward Bill Bradley had an idea. Put in our best shooters, he suggested. If Chamberlain stayed under the basket, the Knicks would have open shots. If he came out, the Knicks would make quick passes until they found an open man. The tactic worked. The Knicks outscored the Lakers 32–18 in the fourth quarter. They won 107–100. "The fifth game," said forward Dave DeBusschere, "was one of the greatest basketball games ever played."

DAVE DeBUSSCHERE made the All-Defensive First Team six times.

Walt "Clyde" Frazier quarterbacked the team. The Knicks surged to a
60–22 mark. They met the Lakers in the NBA Finals. The Lakers had a
trio of superstars: Wilt Chamberlain, Jerry West, and Elgin Baylor. They
combined for an average of 83 points a game in the regular season.
The Knicks fought tooth and nail. They forced the Lakers to seven
games. New York won one of the most memorable championship
series of all time.

The Knicks continued playing at a high level. Returned to
health after a back injury, forward Phil Jackson became a key component
of the team. They reached the Eastern Conference finals the following
season, and then lost the NBA Finals to the Lakers in 1972. "Playing
basketball [under Holzman] became more fun than I had ever imagined,"
said Bradley. It became even more fun in 1973. The Knicks trounced
the Lakers four games to one to win the NBA championship again. It

WILLIAM "RED" HOLZMAN was the winningest coach in franchise history.

was their second title in four years. "The Knicks are so well-balanced,"
Chamberlain said, "and have tremendous passing and so many good
shooters that you can't concentrate on one man."

New York hoped for a repeat championship in 1974. But several players
were now aging. They still managed to advance to the conference finals.
There they lost to Boston, four games to one. Reed retired after the
season. Without him, the Knicks fell to 40–42 in 1974–75. It was their
first losing mark in eight years. Remarkably, they still made the playoffs.
But they were knocked out in the first round. They did slightly worse the
following season, winning just 38 games.

LEGENDS OF THE HARDWOOD

CLYDE

WALT "CLYDE" FRAZIER, POINT GUARD, 6-FOOT-4, 1967-77

Walt Frazier was the Knicks' top draft choice in 1967. "I really played lousy at first," he said. Then Red Holzman took over as coach. Holzman emphasized defense. Frazier was a defense-first player. He flourished in Holzman's system. The movie *Bonnie and Clyde* came out during his rookie season. The character Clyde Barrow, played by actor Warren Beatty, was a stylish dresser. So was Frazier. A Knicks trainer nicknamed him "Clyde." Frazier made the All-NBA First Team four times. He was a seven-time All-Star and seven-time All-Defensive First Team selection. Teammate Willis Reed praised Frazier's leadership qualities. "It's Clyde's ball," Reed said. "He just lets us play with it once in a while."

24

THE EWING ERA BEGINS

It seemed obvious that the team needed new blood. But team officials made one of the worst decisions in franchise history before the 1976–77 season. The rival American Basketball Association (ABA) had stopped playing. Four of its teams joined the NBA.

Guard **EARL "THE PEARL" MONROE** had a feathery jump shot and flashy moves.

Explosive forward **BERNARD KING** was nearly impossible for opponents to defend.

"HE'S LIKE A BIRD," SAID NEW COACH HUBIE BROWN ABOUT KING. "HE SWOOPS TOWARD THE BASKET AND SEEMS TO BE DESCENDING. THEN, AT THE LAST INSTANT, HE ELEVATES, AND YOU'LL SEE AN INCREDIBLE MOVE."

One was the New York Nets. The Knicks demanded that the Nets pay them $4.8 million. They said the Nets were "invading" the Knicks' territory. The Nets had already paid more than $3 million to join the league. They didn't want to pay the Knicks, too. Instead, the Nets offered the Knicks highflying forward Julius "Dr. J" Erving. Erving was a prolific scorer. Yet the Knicks said no. The Philadelphia 76ers bought his contract instead. The 76ers advanced to the NBA Finals four times before Dr. J retired in 1987. He ended his career with more than 30,000 points. During that same time frame, the Knicks had seven losing seasons. They did advance to the conference semifinals three times before bowing out. Two of those defeats came at the hands of Dr. J and the 76ers.

much of the Knicks' limited success was thanks to small forward Bernard King. He joined the team in 1982. "He's like a bird," said new coach Hubie Brown. "He swoops toward the

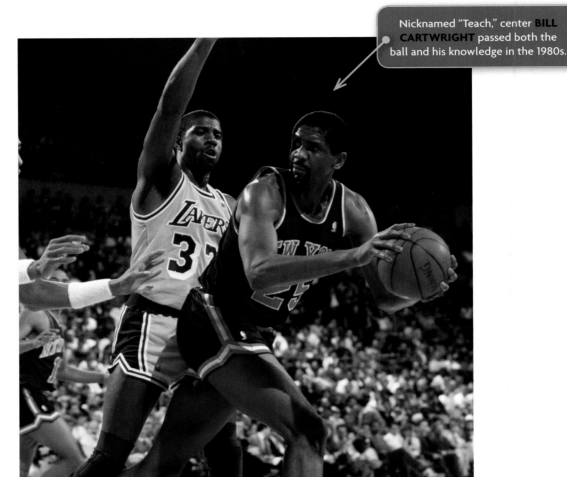

Nicknamed "Teach," center **BILL CARTWRIGHT** passed both the ball and his knowledge in the 1980s.

basket and seems to be descending. Then, at the last instant, he elevates, and you'll see an incredible move." King led the league in scoring in 1984–85. He averaged nearly 33 points a game. Unfortunately, he suffered a severe knee injury late that season. The Knicks finished 24–58. It was their worst record in more than 20 years.

Then the Knicks benefited from some good luck. In previous years, the teams with the worst record in each conference flipped a coin. The winner had the first choice in the NBA Draft. That changed in 1985. The NBA began a lottery system. Teams that didn't qualify for the playoffs held a drawing. The winner of the drawing would have the first choice.

MOTOR CITY MADNESS

NBA PLAYOFFS, GAME 5 OF THE FIRST ROUND, NEW YORK KNICKS AT DETROIT PISTONS, APRIL 27, 1984

Everyone was hot when the air conditioning in Detroit's Joe Louis Arena broke down. No one was hotter than the Pistons' Isiah Thomas and the Knicks' Bernard King. Thomas drained 16 points in the final 93 seconds. That tied the score and forced overtime. King had a severe case of the flu. Both his middle fingers were dislocated. Yet he scored 44 points. With seconds remaining, New York clung to a two-point lead. A Knicks player missed a shot. King soared over four Pistons players and two teammates. He snagged the rebound and slammed the ball through the hoop. The Knicks won, 127–123. "I probably never jumped that high before in my life," King said.

PATRICK EWING'S exciting play brought fans back to Madison Square Garden.

"NOT SINCE LEW ALCINDOR [KAREEM ABDUL-JABBAR] LEFT UCLA IN 1969 HAD THERE BEEN A GIANT AS DOMINANT AS THE 7-FOOT, 240-POUND EWING," OBSERVED SPORTSWRITER CHRIS BALLARD.

n 1985, there was no question as to who that choice would be: Patrick Ewing. "Not since Lew Alcindor [Kareem Abdul-Jabbar] left UCLA in 1969 had there been a giant as dominant as the 7-foot, 240-pound Ewing," observed sportswriter Chris Ballard. "In four years at Georgetown, Ewing took the Hoyas to three NCAA finals, winning one. He offered the total package. He could score in the post, defend, rebound, and knock down an 18-foot jumper." He also had a scowling "game face" that often frightened his opponents. The Knicks won the drawing. Ewing immediately lived up to expectations. He averaged 20 points and 9 rebounds a game. He was named Rookie of the Year. The Knicks didn't play as well. They won only 23 games that season. The losing continued in the next two seasons. But things were about to get better.

Guard **JOHN STARKS** is known for "The Dunk," a last-minute shot during the 1993 playoffs.

A LONG RUN
OF SUCCESS

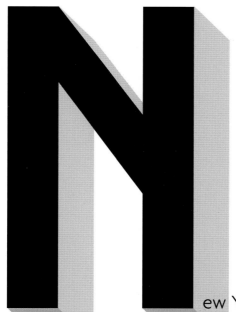ew York added point guard Mark Jackson in the 1987 Draft. He averaged nearly 14 points and 11 assists a game. He was named Rookie of the Year. The Knicks made the playoffs,

Forward **ANTHONY MASON** received the NBA's Sixth Man of the Year award in 1994–95.

though they lost in the first round. Adding other players such as bruising forward Charles Oakley helped the Knicks become a regular in successive playoffs. Another important addition was legendary coach Pat Riley in 1991. He won four NBA titles with the Lakers in the 1980s. "The Knicks would never be the Lakers, but by unleashing the snarling talents of guys like [forward Anthony] Mason and [guard John] Starks, Riley got them good fast," said sportswriter Mark Kriegel. "What they lacked in talent, they made up in heart, hustle, and hard work."

The Knicks reached the NBA Finals in 1994. They took a 3–2 lead over the Houston Rockets. But they didn't shoot well in the next two games. They also had a hard time getting the ball inside to Ewing. The Rockets won both games and the title. Riley also guided the team to two Eastern Conference finals. But he wanted more power and money than the team was willing to give him. He moved on to coach the Miami Heat in 1995.

The Knicks continued to play well after Riley left. They made it to the conference semifinals the next three seasons. Most people didn't think much of the team's chances in the strike-shortened 1998–99 season. New York went just 27–23. It barely qualified for the playoffs. But then everything seemed to come together. New York beat top-seeded Miami on a last-second shot by guard Allan Houston in the decisive Game 5. The Knicks swept the Atlanta Hawks in the second round. Early in

36

DOLLAR BILL TO PRESIDENT BRADLEY?

BILL BRADLEY, SMALL FORWARD, 6-FOOT-5, 1967–77

"Dollar Bill" Bradley was one of the smartest people to play in the NBA. He didn't join the Knicks the year he was drafted. Instead he chose to study in England for two years. When he began playing, he helped the team win its only two NBA championships. A few months after retiring, Bradley ran for the U.S. Senate from New Jersey. He won. He was re-elected twice. Every Labor Day weekend, he walked nearly 130 miles (209 km) to meet voters. In 2000, he ran for the Democratic presidential nomination. Al Gore was the only other Democratic candidate. Gore won the first 20 primaries. Bradley dropped out of the race.

> "PATRICK IS A CHAMPION, EVEN IF HE HASN'T WON A CHAMPIONSHIP YET," SAID COACH JEFF VAN GUNDY. "HE PRACTICED AND PLAYED LIKE A CHAMPION EACH DAY HE WAS HERE."

the conference finals against the Indiana Pacers, Ewing suffered a torn Achilles tendon. New York overcame the loss of Ewing. It won the series, four games to two. But without Ewing, it lost the Finals to the powerful San Antonio Spurs.

The Knicks reached the conference finals the following year. Again, they faced Indiana. The Pacers turned the tables this time. They took the series four games to two. Team officials decided they couldn't win a championship with Ewing. They traded him. They praised him for his contributions to the team. "Patrick is a champion, even if he hasn't won a championship yet," said coach Jeff Van Gundy. "He practiced and played like a champion each day he was here."

38

A LONG DRY SPELL

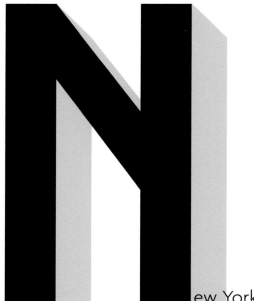

New York didn't play like a champion after Ewing's departure. It did win 48 games in 2000–01. But it lost in the first round of the playoffs. The Knicks tumbled to 30 wins the following season.

THE NBA: A HISTORY OF HOOPS

39

ALLAN HOUSTON'S last-second shot kept the Knicks alive in the 1999 postseason.

LINSANITY

JEREMY LIN, POINT GUARD, 6-FOOT-3, 2011–12

The Houston Rockets cut Jeremy Lin on December 24, 2011. The Knicks signed him three days later. No one expected much. He hardly played for more than a month. Coach Mike D'Antoni finally let Lin start. Lin scored 25 points. He netted 28 in the next game, then 23, then 38. The Knicks won all four games. A few days later, Lin sank a desperation three-point shot to win yet another game. Metta World Peace of the Lakers had watched the game. He yelled "Linsanity! Linsanity!" as he ran by reporters. The combination of "Lin" and "insanity" stuck. After the season, Lin returned to the Rockets.

LEGENDS OF THE HARDWOOD

Forward **CARMELO ANTHONY** led the NBA with 28.7 points per game in 2012–13.

41

...t was the first time in 14 years that they hadn't qualified for the playoffs. That began a series of trades that confused fans and resulted in steady losses on the court. New York didn't have a winning record for the next eight seasons. The team continued to trade for expensive players who didn't produce on the court.

The Knicks finally made a good personnel move before the 2010–11 season. They signed All-Star power forward Amar'e Stoudemire. "We have taken a big step with Amar'e and we will take another big step, whether that is today or tomorrow or six months from now," said coach Mike D'Antoni. "Another big step" came a few months later. New York made a blockbuster trade with the Denver Nuggets for superstar forward Carmelo Anthony. "At 26 years old, Carmelo is in the prime of his NBA

Big man **AMAR'E STOUDEMIRE** brought energy and excitement to the Knicks.

42

career, having already established himself as one of the game's elite players, and the opportunity to add him to our roster was one we could not pass up," said Knicks president Donnie Walsh. "I feel we now have a great frontcourt tandem in Amar'e and Carmelo." The Knicks had winning records for the next three years. The 2011–12 season was highlighted by guard Jeremy Lin and "Linsanity." The Knicks advanced to the conference semifinals in 2013. They lost again to the Pacers, 4–2.

43

Rookie forward **KRISTAPS PORZINGIS** piled up points and rebounds in 2015–16.

Signed in 2016, point guard **DERRICK ROSE** possessed a combination of speed and size.

T hey couldn't maintain the momentum. The Knicks won only 37 games in 2013–14. The wheels all came off the following season. They had a franchise-worst 17–65 record. The team did a little better in 2015–16. It won 32 games. Seven-foot-3 rookie power forward Kristaps Porzingis made an impressive debut. He averaged 14 points, 7 rebounds, and 2 blocked shots a game. "At some point in time, he's just going to be phenomenal," said new coach Kurt Rambis. "We think eventually he's going to be unstoppable. He's going to create a tremendous matchup problem for teams." Another key pickup was veteran shooting guard Arron Afflalo. He was the team's third-leading scorer, with nearly 13 points a game. But the Knicks struggled in 2016–17. A trade for star point guard Derrick Rose didn't go as well as expected. The team also had personnel issues on and off the court. New York finished just 31–51.

The Knicks have an interesting pattern of wins and losses. They did very well in the 1950s, the 1970s, and the 1990s. If this pattern continues, the 2010s should be good as well. The decade began well, though the recent seasons have been somewhat of a letdown. Fans hope the team will return to its previous winning form and add another championship banner to the two they already have.

SELECTED BIBLIOGRAPHY

Ballard, Chris. *The Art of a Beautiful Game: The Thinking Fan's Tour of the NBA*. New York: Simon & Schuster, 2010.

Hareas, John. *Ultimate Basketball: More Than 100 Years of the Sport's Evolution*. New York: DK, 2004.

Hubbard, Jan, ed. *The Official NBA Basketball Encyclopedia*. 3rd edition. New York: Doubleday, 2000.

NBA.com. "New York Knicks." http://www.nba.com/knicks.

Simmons, Bill. *The Book of Basketball: The NBA According to the Sports Guy*. New York: Ballantine, 2009.

Sports Illustrated. *Sports Illustrated Basketball's Greatest*. New York: Sports Illustrated, 2014.

WEBSITES

1970 NBA FINALS

https://www.youtube.com/watch?v=2UiNIVqU5po

Watch a video about Willis Reed's 1970 Finals injury and his determination to play in the deciding Game 7.

JR. NBA

http://jr.nba.com/

This kids site has games, videos, game results, team and player information, statistics, and more.

Note: Every effort has been made to ensure that any websites listed above were active at the time of publication. However, because of the nature of the Internet, it is impossible to guarantee that these sites will remain active indefinitely or that their contents will not be altered.

INDEX

48